Preface

The IGNOU MCS-203: Operating System course is a vital part of the Post Graduate Diploma in Computer Applications (PGDCA) curriculum. It lays the foundation for understanding the core functions of operating systems, such as process management, memory allocation, file systems, CPU scheduling, and security. These concepts are critical for students who aim to build a strong career in computer science and information technology.

This book, IGNOU MCS-203: Operating System Previous Years Unsolved Papers, has been compiled to provide students with an invaluable resource for their exam preparation. It brings together a collection of previous years' unsolved question papers, offering students the opportunity to practice, assess their knowledge, and develop problem-solving strategies. These unsolved papers are an excellent way to strengthen the understanding of operating system fundamentals and prepare for the types of questions likely to appear in exams.

The focus of this book is to encourage self-study and independent thinking. By working through these papers, students will gain a clearer understanding of key operating system topics, improve their analytical skills, and become familiar with the exam format. We believe this compilation will help students achieve academic success and build a strong foundation in operating systems.
We hope this book serves as a valuable tool for students and aids them in their journey toward academic and professional success.

Table of Contents

MCS – 203

Post Graduate Diploma in Computer Applications (PGDCA)
Chapter 1: Term-End Examination, December, 2021
MCS-203: Operating Systems

Time: 3 Hours
Maximum Marks: 100
Weightage: 70%

Note: (i) Question No. **1** is compulsory.
(ii) Attempt any **three** questions from the rest.

1. (a) Discuss SCAN and C-SCAN disk scheduling algorithms. List the advantages of SCAN over C-SCAN algorithm. 10

(b) Consider the following reference-string : 10

1, 2, 3, 4, 2, 1, 5, 6, 2, 1, 2, 3, 7, 6

How many page faults would occur for the following algorithms, assuming memory with three frames:

(i) LRU
(ii) Optimal Replacement

(c) List and explain various commonly used directories in iOS. Also mention the purpose of iCloud container of iOS along with its contents. 10

(d) Explain demand paging and memory compression in memory management of WINDOWS-10 O/S. 10

2. (a) Define paged-segmentation and segmented paging. Explain the working principle of paged-segmentation. 10

(b) Explain the memory management in LINUX. 10

3. (a) Write and explain Ricart and Agrawala's mutual exclusion algorithm for distributed systems. 10

(b) Using semaphore, write an algorithm that solves the producer/consumer's problem with a bounded buffer. 10

4. (a) Briefly explain file management system of WINDOWS 10 O/S. 10

(b) Explain the security features in LINUX with respect to user accounts, file permissions, data verification and encrypted storage. 10

5. Write short notes on any four of the following : 4×5=20

(a) Salient features of Android OS

(b) Evolution of iOS

(c) Comparative chart of Symbian, Android with respect to the features :
OS family, user interface, app stores, licence policy, security, voice assistant and power management.

(d) KaiOS

(e) Any five design issues involved in distributed systems.

MCS – 203

Post Graduate Diploma in Computer Applications (PGDCA)
Chapter 2: Term-End Examination, June, 2022
MCS-203: Operating Systems

Time: 3 Hours
Maximum Marks: 100
Weightage: 70%

Note: Question No. **1** is **compulsory.** Attempt any **three** questions from the rest.

1. (a) Define a Deadlock. Explain the necessary and sufficient conditions for a deadlock occurrence. Also explain how it can be prevented. 10

(b) Write and explain the Lamport's Scheme of Ordering of Events in Distributed Systems. 10

(c) Explain the file management system in iOS and also briefly mention the security aspects of file system. 10

(d) Describe briefly Virtual Memory Organization and Demand Paging in WINDOWS-10. 10

2. (a) Discuss briefly the following Scheduling algorithms : 10
(i) FCFS
(ii) Round Robin
(iii) Priority-based Scheduling
Explain the difference in the degree to which the above scheduling algorithms discriminate in favour of short processes.

(b) Briefly explain the two non-contiguous disk storage allocation schemes, with the help of an illustration for each. 10

3. (a) Describe the process management in LINUX, which includes process priorities, process hierarchy, process states and threads management. 10

(b) With the help of a simple block diagram, explain the XNU kernel architecture which was initially used for Mac OS. 10

4. (a) Define Segmentation Scheme. With the help of a diagram, explain the principles of its operation. 10

(b) Define Thrashing and explain the reason of its occurrence, with the help of an example. Describe briefly the techniques of prevention of thrashing. 10

5. (a) What is a Semaphore ? Give solution to the Sleeping Barber Problem using Semaphore. 10

(b) List the contents of a Process Control Block (PCB). Explain the significance of each of its components. 10

Post Graduate Diploma in Computer Applications (PGDCA)
Chapter 2: Term-End Examination, December, 2022
MCS-203 : Operating Systems

Time: 3 Hours
Maximum Marks: 100
Weightage: 70%

Note: Question No. **1** is compulsory and carries 40 marks. Attempt any **three** questions from remaining Questions No. **2** to Question No. **5**.

1. (a) What are concurrent processes ? Write Dekker's solution for mutual exclusion and explain it. 10

(b) Consider the following set of processes, with the length of CPU burst time given in milliseconds: 10

Process	CPU burst time
P1	10
P2	8
P3	4
P4	6

All the four processes (P1, P2, P3, P4) arrived at the same time in the order P1, P2, P3 and P4. Draw Gantt charts illustrating the execution of the processes using SJF, FCFS and RR (Quantum = 2) scheduling. What is the turnaround time of each process for each of the scheduling algorithms ? Also find the average waiting time for each of the processes.

(c) Define virtual memory. Explain the principles of operation and the address mapping scheme of it. Also, write briefly about the protection and sharing in virtual memory. 10

(d) With reference to Android operating system explain the layered architecture and its components. Also draw the layered architecture diagram indicating its components. 10

2. (a) Describe the difference between security policy vs. security model in the context of operating system. Briefly explain the following security models : 10

    (i) Access Matrix Model
    (ii) Discretionary Access Control

(b) With the help of an example, explain the linked/chained allocation scheme of non-contiguous memory allocation. 10

3. (a) Define an overlay with the help of an example. Explain the allocation scheme using overlays. How is this scheme different from swapping ? 10

(b) Define deadlock. List and explain four necessary conditions that must hold simultaneously for a deadlock to occur. 10

4. (a) When does a page fault occur in demand paging ? Describe the action taken by the operating system when it occurs. 10

(b) What is Disk Scheduling ? With the help of an example for each, explain the following disk scheduling algorithms :

10

(i) FCFS

(ii) SSTF

5. Write short notes on any four of the following : $4 \times 5 = 20$

(a) Process and thread management in iOS

(b) IPC mechanisms in Android

(c) File permissions, data verification, encrypted storage and remote access in Linux operating system.

(d) Inter-process communication in Windows 10

(e) File management in LINUX operating system

Chapter 4: Most Asked Important Questions - Part A

Q.1. Explain the concept of deadlock in operating systems. Discuss the necessary conditions for deadlock and explain how a resource allocation graph can be used to detect a deadlock.

Answer: A deadlock occurs when a set of processes are blocked because each process is holding a resource and waiting for another resource acquired by some other process. Coffman's conditions for deadlock are:

1) Mutual Exclusion: at least one resource must be held in a non-shareable mode.
2) Hold and Wait: a process holding a resource can request additional resources.
3) No Preemption: resources cannot be forcibly taken from processes.
4) Circular Wait: a closed chain exists where each process waits for a resource held by the next process.

A resource allocation graph (RAG) can be used to detect deadlocks. In the RAG, processes are represented as circles and resources as squares. A directed edge from process to resource indicates a request, and an edge from resource to process indicates allocation. If the RAG contains a cycle and each resource has only one instance, then a deadlock exists.

Q.2. Define and explain virtual memory. Describe the concept of paging and page replacement algorithms.

Answer: Virtual memory is a memory management technique that enables a process to execute without having its entire code and data in physical memory. It allows processes to use more memory than the actual RAM by using secondary storage. Paging divides physical memory into fixed-size blocks called frames and divides logical memory into pages of the same size. The operating system maintains a page table to map virtual addresses to physical addresses. Page replacement algorithms are used when a page fault occurs, and memory is full. Algorithms include FIFO (First-In-First-Out), LRU (Least Recently Used), and Optimal Page Replacement. FIFO replaces the oldest page in memory, LRU replaces the page not used for the longest time, and Optimal replaces the page that will not be used for the longest time in the future.

Q.3. What is process scheduling? Describe First-Come-First-Serve (FCFS), Shortest Job First (SJF), and Round Robin (RR) scheduling algorithms with examples.

Answer: Process scheduling is the mechanism by which the operating system selects a process from the ready queue to execute on the CPU. FCFS scheduling executes processes in the order of arrival, which may lead to the convoy effect. SJF selects the process with the shortest burst time, minimizing average waiting time but causing starvation for longer processes. RR uses a time quantum to switch between processes in a cyclic order, ensuring fairness and responsiveness. Example: Given processes P1(5ms), P2(3ms), and P3(8ms), FCFS may produce a Gantt chart showing P1→P2→P3, SJF would execute P2→P1→P3, and RR with a time quantum of 2ms would distribute CPU time among all processes in cycles.

Q.4. Describe semaphores. Illustrate how semaphores can be used to solve the producer-consumer problem.

Answer: A semaphore is an integer variable used for process synchronization in concurrent systems. It has two atomic operations: wait (P) decrements the semaphore and blocks if the value is negative, and signal (V) increments the semaphore and wakes up blocked processes if necessary. In the producer-consumer problem, semaphores are used to synchronize access to a bounded buffer. Three semaphores are used: empty (initially set to the size of the buffer), full (initially 0), and mutex (initially 1). The producer waits on empty and mutex before adding an item, then signals mutex and full. The consumer waits on full and mutex before removing an item, then signals mutex and empty.

Q.5. Explain the architecture of Linux operating system with a neat diagram.

Answer: Linux follows a monolithic architecture where the kernel provides direct services to user applications. The architecture consists of user space and kernel space. User space contains applications, shells, and libraries, while kernel space includes the process scheduler, memory manager, virtual file system (VFS), device drivers, and network stack. The kernel manages hardware abstraction and system calls. The process scheduler enables multitasking, memory management handles virtual memory and paging, the VFS provides a common interface for different file systems, and device drivers enable hardware communication. A diagram should illustrate the separation of user and kernel spaces with modules such as process management, memory management, file system, and drivers under the kernel.

Q.6. Explain paging and segmentation. Compare their advantages and disadvantages.
Answer: Paging divides the physical memory into fixed-size blocks called frames and divides logical memory into blocks of the same size called pages. A page table maps virtual pages to physical frames. Advantages of paging include elimination of external fragmentation and ease of memory allocation, but it causes internal fragmentation when the last page is not fully utilized. Segmentation divides memory into variable-sized logical segments such as code, stack, and data, which reflects the logical structure of a program. Segmentation is more flexible and provides better protection but suffers from external fragmentation and requires complex memory management.

Q.7. What are the various process states? Explain process state transitions with a diagram.
Answer: The process states are: New (process is being created), Ready (waiting for CPU), Running (executing), Waiting (blocked for an event), and Terminated (finished execution). Transitions include: New → Ready (admitted), Ready → Running (scheduler dispatch), Running → Waiting (I/O request), Waiting → Ready (I/O completion), Running → Ready (preemption), and Running → Terminated (exit). A state diagram illustrates these transitions with arrows showing movement between states.

Q.8. What are deadlock prevention, avoidance, and detection techniques? Explain each with examples.
Answer: Deadlock prevention ensures at least one of Coffman's conditions cannot hold, e.g., disallowing hold-and-wait by requiring all resources to be requested at once. Deadlock avoidance dynamically checks resource allocation requests using algorithms like Banker's Algorithm, which grants requests only if the system remains in a safe state. Deadlock detection allows deadlocks to occur and periodically runs detection algorithms (e.g., resource allocation graphs) to identify deadlocks. Recovery involves aborting processes or preempting resources.

Q.9. Define a thread. Differentiate between user-level and kernel-level threads.

Answer: A thread is the smallest unit of CPU execution within a process. User-level threads are managed by user-level libraries and the OS kernel is unaware of them, making them fast but lacking kernel-level concurrency. Kernel-level threads are managed by the OS and allow true parallelism on multiprocessor systems but involve higher overhead due to kernel intervention.

Q.10. Explain the concept of context switching. Why is it important? What overheads are involved in context switching?

Answer: Context switching is the process of saving the state of a currently running process and restoring the state of another process so that the CPU can switch to it. It is important for multitasking and CPU sharing among processes. The overhead includes saving/restoring registers, program counter, and memory maps, which does not contribute to useful computation and can affect system performance.

Q.11. Discuss the concept of process synchronization. Explain Peterson's algorithm for mutual exclusion.

Answer: Process synchronization ensures that multiple processes can safely access shared resources without data inconsistencies. Peterson's algorithm achieves mutual exclusion for two processes by using two shared variables: a boolean array flag[2] and an integer turn. Each process sets its flag to true and sets turn to the other process. It then waits until either the other process's flag is false or it is its turn. This algorithm ensures mutual exclusion and progress but works only for two processes.

Q.12. What is the difference between preemptive and non-preemptive scheduling? Give examples of each.

Answer: Preemptive scheduling allows the OS to suspend a running process and assign CPU to another process (e.g., Round Robin, Priority Scheduling). Non-preemptive scheduling does not allow a running process to be interrupted; it runs until completion or blocking (e.g., FCFS, SJF without preemption). Preemptive scheduling improves CPU utilization and responsiveness but requires context switching.

Q.13. Explain demand paging with the help of a diagram. What is a page fault? How is it handled?

Answer: Demand paging loads pages into memory only when they are needed. Initially, none of the process's pages are in RAM; accessing a page not in memory causes a page fault. The OS handles the page fault by locating the page on disk, bringing it into RAM, updating the page table, and restarting the process. A diagram shows a logical address being mapped to a page table, and the page fault handler fetching the page.

Q.14. Explain multilevel feedback queue scheduling with an example.

Answer: Multilevel feedback queues use multiple queues with different priorities and scheduling algorithms. A process starts in a high-priority queue; if it uses too much CPU time, it is demoted to a lower-priority queue. For example, processes P1 and P2 may start in Q1 (Round Robin, quantum=5), but if they exceed their quantum, they move to Q2 (longer quantum or FCFS). This approach balances responsiveness for interactive tasks and fairness for CPU-bound jobs.

Q.15. Describe the architecture of Android operating system.

Answer: Android architecture consists of four layers:

1. **Linux Kernel**: Hardware abstraction, memory management, process management.
2. **Libraries and Android Runtime**: Includes libc, WebKit, SQLite, and ART (Android Runtime).
3. **Application Framework**: Provides APIs for managing resources and UI components.
4. **Applications**: User-installed apps and built-in apps like dialer, browser. A block diagram illustrates these layers with arrows showing their interaction.

Q.16. What are the advantages and disadvantages of multiprogramming?

Answer: Advantages include increased CPU utilization, better system throughput, and reduced idle time. Disadvantages are increased complexity in OS design, potential for deadlocks, and challenges in memory management due to multiple concurrent processes.

Q.17. Discuss the differences between monolithic, layered, and microkernel operating systems.

Answer: In a monolithic OS (e.g., Linux), all OS services run in kernel space. Layered OS (e.g., THE) organizes services hierarchically for better modularity and debugging. Microkernel OS (e.g., Minix) runs only essential services (like IPC and basic scheduling) in kernel space, with other services in user space for better reliability and security.

Q.18. Explain disk scheduling algorithms with examples of SSTF and SCAN.
Answer: SSTF (Shortest Seek Time First) services requests closest to the current head position. SCAN moves the disk arm in one direction servicing requests until the end is reached, then reverses. Example: For requests at 98, 183, 37, 122, 14, 124 with head at 53, SSTF serves 37 first (closest), then 14, 98, and so on. SCAN would move in one direction (e.g., towards 0), servicing all requests, then reverse.

Q.19. Explain the concept of file systems. Compare contiguous, linked, and indexed allocation.
Answer: A file system organizes and stores files on storage devices.

1. **Contiguous allocation**: Stores files in contiguous blocks; simple but suffers from external fragmentation.
2. **Linked allocation**: Each block points to the next; no fragmentation but poor random access.
3. **Indexed allocation**: Uses an index block to store pointers to file blocks; supports random access but overhead of index block.

Q.20. What are the goals and functions of an operating system?
Answer: The operating system (OS) is system software that acts as an intermediary between computer hardware and the user. It manages hardware resources and provides an environment where applications can run effectively. The primary goals of an OS are:
(1) **Convenience**: To make computer use more user-friendly.
(2) **Efficiency**: To manage resources efficiently and maximize system utilization.
(3) **Ability to evolve**: To provide an environment where new functionalities and services can be added.

Functions of an OS include:

1. **Process Management**: Creates, schedules, and terminates processes. It handles process synchronization, communication, and deadlock handling.

2. **Memory Management**: Allocates and deallocates memory to processes, maintains memory protection, and handles virtual memory and paging.

3. **File System Management**: Organizes and manages data storage on devices; supports access methods, directories, and file security.

4. **Device Management**: Controls and coordinates I/O devices using drivers and manages buffering, caching, and spooling.

5. **Security and Protection**: Prevents unauthorized access to resources, enforces user authentication and data integrity.

6. **User Interface**: Provides CLI (command-line interface) or GUI (graphical user interface) for interaction with the system.

Q.21. What is mutual exclusion? Explain the critical section problem and describe Dekker's algorithm for two processes.

Answer: Mutual exclusion is a property ensuring that only one process enters its critical section at a time, preventing data inconsistency when accessing shared resources. The **critical section problem** involves designing protocols that enforce mutual exclusion, progress, and bounded waiting.

Dekker's Algorithm solves this for two processes using:

(1) **Flag array** where each process indicates interest,.

(2) A **turn variable** to resolve conflicts. Each process sets its flag and assigns the turn to the other process; it then waits until the other process is not interested or it's its turn. This ensures no two processes enter their critical sections simultaneously and avoids deadlock and starvation.

Q.22. Explain inter-process communication (IPC). Describe shared memory and message passing techniques.

Answer: IPC allows processes to communicate and synchronize their actions.
1. Shared Memory: Processes share a region of memory; synchronization primitives like semaphores ensure data consistency. It offers high speed but requires explicit synchronization.
2. Message Passing: Processes exchange data via messages using send/receive operations. It can

be **direct** (processes communicate directly) or **indirect** (via mailboxes). It is safer for distributed systems but incurs more overhead due to kernel intervention.

Q.23. What are the different types of operating systems? Explain batch, multiprogramming, and real-time systems.

Answer: Types of OS:

1. **Batch OS**: Jobs with similar needs are grouped and processed without user interaction; suitable for tasks like payroll systems.
2. **Multiprogramming OS**: Allows multiple programs in memory to improve CPU utilization; the OS switches CPU between jobs.
3. **Real-Time OS**: Processes data as it comes in within strict time constraints. **Hard RTOS** misses deadlines are catastrophic (e.g., avionics); **Soft RTOS** tolerates occasional delays (e.g., video streaming).

Q.24. Explain disk management and describe free space management techniques.

Answer: Disk management involves allocation, scheduling, and tracking free storage. **Free space management techniques:**

1. **Bitmaps**: Each bit represents a disk block (0 = free, 1 = occupied). Simple but requires scanning for allocation.
2. **Linked List**: Free blocks are linked together; allocation requires traversing the list.
3. **Grouping**: Free blocks are stored in groups; the first block contains pointers to the next free blocks.
4. **Counting**: Maintains the starting address and count of free consecutive blocks. Efficient for large contiguous free spaces.

Q.25. What are real-time operating systems (RTOS)? Discuss their characteristics and types.

Answer: RTOS is designed for systems that require precise timing and predictable behavior. **Characteristics:** Deterministic scheduling, low latency, minimal jitter, and priority-based task handling.

Types:

1. **Hard RTOS**: Strict timing requirements; failure leads to system failure (e.g., pacemakers).

2. **Soft RTOS**: Flexible timing requirements; occasional misses are acceptable (e.g., audio/video playback).

Q.26. Describe the architecture and components of Windows operating system.
Answer: Windows OS has a layered architecture:

1. **Hardware Abstraction Layer (HAL):** Provides hardware independence.
2. **Kernel Mode:** Includes microkernel for scheduling, process/thread management, memory management, I/O handling.
3. **User Mode:** Comprises environment subsystems (e.g., Win32), system libraries, and user applications.

Q.27. What is a race condition? Explain with an example. How can it be avoided?

Answer: A race condition occurs when the output depends on the sequence of execution of processes accessing shared resources. Example: Two threads incrementing a counter simultaneously may overwrite each other's results.
Avoidance: Use synchronization techniques like mutexes, semaphores, or monitors to serialize access to shared resources.

Q.28. Explain the Readers-Writers problem and provide a semaphore-based solution.

Answer: Multiple readers can access a resource simultaneously, but writers require exclusive access.

Solution: Use semaphores readCount, mutex, and wrt. Readers increment readCount under mutex; if it's the first reader, they wait on wrt. Writers wait on wrt before writing. On exit, readers decrement readCount and signal wrt if no readers remain.

Q.29. Discuss memory management techniques: fixed partitioning, dynamic partitioning, and paging.

Answer:

1. **Fixed Partitioning:** Divides memory into fixed-size partitions; may cause internal fragmentation.

2. Dynamic Partitioning: Allocates memory as per process needs; leads to external fragmentation.

3. Paging: Divides memory into fixed-size pages and frames; eliminates external fragmentation but can cause internal fragmentation.

Q.30. Explain thrashing in operating systems. How can it be prevented?

Answer: Thrashing happens when excessive paging activity causes low CPU utilization because processes spend more time swapping pages than executing.

Prevention: Use the **working set model** to keep active pages in memory, increase physical memory, or apply load control to limit multiprogramming level.

Q31. Explain the directory structure of file systems. Describe different types of directory structures in detail with examples.

Answer: A **directory structure** organizes and maintains information about all files in a file system. It keeps track of the location, size, and access rights of files.

Types of Directory Structures:

1. Single-Level Directory:

a. All files are contained in the same directory.

b. Example: Early MS-DOS systems.

c. Advantage: Simple and easy to implement.

d. Disadvantage: File name collisions and no support for grouping.

2. Two-Level Directory:

a. Each user has their own directory under a master directory.

b. Example: UNIX /home/username.

c. Advantage: Users can have files with the same names.

d. Disadvantage: Difficult to organize large projects.

3. Tree-Structured Directory:

a. Directories form a tree; users can create subdirectories and organize files hierarchically.

b. Example: Windows directory structure (C:\Users\Documents).

c. Advantage: Supports file grouping and easy navigation.

4. Acyclic Graph Directory:

a. Allows shared subdirectories or files by using links.

b. Example: Symbolic links in UNIX systems.

5. General Graph Directory:

a. Similar to acyclic graph but allows cycles; requires garbage collection.

Conclusion: Tree-structured directories are most common in modern systems as they balance simplicity and flexibility.

Q32. What is file allocation? Explain the different file allocation methods in detail with their advantages and disadvantages.

Answer:

File allocation refers to the method used by the operating system to store files on disk and manage space efficiently.

Types of File Allocation:

1. Contiguous Allocation:

In contiguous allocation, files occupy a set of blocks that are stored sequentially on the disk. For example, a file requiring five blocks would be stored from block 10 to block 14 in a continuous sequence. This method has the advantage of fast access because all blocks are stored in order, making sequential reading very efficient. However, it suffers from external fragmentation, and resizing a file can be problematic if there is no adjacent free space available.

2. Linked Allocation:

In linked allocation, each file is stored as a linked list of disk blocks where each block contains a pointer to the next block. This approach eliminates external fragmentation and allows files to grow easily without needing contiguous space. The disadvantage is that random access becomes inefficient because to access a particular block, the system must traverse all preceding blocks. It also requires additional storage space for maintaining the pointers in each block.

3. Indexed Allocation:

In indexed allocation, an index block is used to store all the pointers to the blocks occupied by a file. For example, UNIX file systems use inodes as index structures for file management. This method supports direct access to file blocks, which makes it efficient for both small and large files.

However, it involves overhead for maintaining the index block, especially when managing very large files that may require multi-level indexing.

Conclusion: Indexed allocation combines the benefits of the other two methods and is widely used in modern file systems.

Q33. Explain the concept of file protection and security. Describe different protection mechanisms provided by operating systems.

Answer: File protection ensures that only authorized users can access or modify files, maintaining data integrity and privacy.

Protection Mechanisms:

1. Access Control Lists (ACLs):

a. Each file has a list specifying access rights (read, write, execute) for each user or group.

b. **Example**: Windows NTFS permissions.

2. User Authentication:

a. Ensures only legitimate users access the system via passwords, biometrics, or tokens.

3. Encryption:

a. Data is encoded so unauthorized users cannot read it even if they gain access.

4. File Permissions:

a. UNIX/Linux uses read (r), write (w), and execute (x) permissions for user, group, and others.

b. Example: chmod 755 filename.

5. Backup and Recovery Mechanisms:

a. Protect against accidental deletion or corruption.

Conclusion: Combining these mechanisms ensures robust file protection in multi-user systems.

Q.34. What is paging? Explain the process of paging in memory management with the help of a diagram.

Answer:

Paging is a memory management scheme that eliminates external fragmentation by dividing physical memory into fixed-size blocks called **frames** and logical memory into blocks of the same size called **pages**.

How Paging Works:

1. **Logical Address Structure:** Consists of a page number and offset.
2. **Page Table:** Maps page numbers to frame numbers in physical memory.
3. **Address Translation:** The CPU generates a logical address which the MMU (Memory Management Unit) translates into a physical address using the page table.

Example Diagram:

Logical Address → [Page Number | Offset]

Page Table → [Frame Number]

Physical Address → [Frame Number | Offset]

Advantages:

a. Eliminates external fragmentation.

b. Simplifies memory allocation.

Disadvantages:

a. May cause internal fragmentation.

b. Overhead of maintaining page tables.

Q.35. Describe in detail how an operating system manages input/output devices.

Answer:

The OS manages I/O devices to provide a consistent interface to applications and ensure efficient sharing of devices.

Key Functions of I/O Management:

1. **Device Drivers:** Translate OS commands into device-specific operations.
2. **Buffering:** Temporarily stores data in memory while transferring between devices to handle speed mismatches.
3. **Caching:** Stores frequently accessed data for faster retrieval.
4. **Spooling:** Overlaps I/O operations with CPU processing (e.g., print spooling).
5. **Error Handling:** Detects and corrects errors during I/O operations.

I/O Control Methods:

1. **Programmed I/O:** CPU actively waits for I/O completion.
2. **Interrupt-Driven I/O:** CPU is interrupted when I/O is complete.

3. **Direct Memory Access (DMA):** Devices transfer data directly to memory without CPU involvement.

Example: In printing, data is spooled into a buffer, allowing the application to continue while the printer completes its job.

Q.36. Explain thrashing in detail. What are its causes and how can it be prevented?

Answer:

Thrashing occurs when a system spends more time swapping pages in and out of memory than executing processes, leading to a severe performance drop.

Causes of Thrashing:

1. High degree of multiprogramming.
2. Processes competing for insufficient physical memory.
3. Poor page replacement policies.

Prevention Techniques:

1. **Working Set Model:** Load only the actively used pages into memory.
2. **Page Fault Frequency (PFF):** Adjust the degree of multiprogramming based on observed page fault rates.
3. **Use of Local Page Replacement:** Allocate a fixed set of frames per process.
4. **Increase Physical Memory:** Reduces page faults.

Conclusion: Proper memory allocation policies and limiting multiprogramming can effectively prevent thrashing.

Q.37. Describe process synchronization and explain semaphore implementation in detail.

Answer:

Process Synchronization is the coordination of processes to ensure safe access to shared resources and avoid data inconsistency.

Semaphore is a synchronization primitive introduced by Dijkstra. It is an integer variable accessed only through two atomic operations:

1. **wait (P):** Decrements semaphore value; if negative, blocks the process.
2. **signal (V):** Increments semaphore value; if the value is non-positive, wakes up a waiting process.

Binary Semaphores (mutex): Used for mutual exclusion.

Counting Semaphores: Used for coordinating access to resources with multiple instances.

Q.38. What is the role of the operating system in ensuring security? Explain authentication and encryption mechanisms.

Answer:

An OS provides security to protect system resources and data from unauthorized access and malicious attacks.

Authentication:

a. Verifies user identity.

b. Methods include passwords, biometric systems (fingerprints, retina scans), and multi-factor authentication (MFA).

Encryption:

a. Protects data confidentiality by converting plain text into cipher text using cryptographic algorithms.

b. Example: SSL/TLS encrypts web communication.

Other Security Features:

1. Firewalls and antivirus software.
2. Access control policies (e.g., RBAC).
3. Secure boot mechanisms.

Q.39. Explain the architecture of the Linux operating system in detail with a diagram.

Answer:

The Linux OS uses a monolithic kernel architecture, combining modularity and performance.

Key Components:

1. User Space: Includes shells, user applications, and system libraries.

2. Kernel Space:

a. Process Management: Schedules and controls process execution.

b. Memory Management: Handles paging, virtual memory, and allocation.

c. File System: Supports multiple file systems (ext4, FAT32).

d. Device Drivers: Interfaces with hardware devices.

e. **Networking Stack:** Implements protocols like TCP/IP.

Text Diagram:

User Applications

|

System Libraries

|

Kernel (Process, Memory, File, Drivers, Network)

|

Hardware

Q.40. Describe the Android operating system architecture and explain the role of each layer.

Answer:

Android is a Linux-based OS designed for mobile devices with a layered architecture:

1. **Linux Kernel:** Provides core system services like security, memory management, and hardware abstraction.
2. **Libraries:** Includes SQLite (database), WebKit (browser engine), and OpenGL ES (graphics).
3. **Android Runtime (ART):** Executes Android apps using ahead-of-time compilation.
4. **Application Framework:** Offers APIs for UI management, activity handling, and resource access.
5. **Applications:** Built-in apps (dialer, browser) and user-installed apps.

Conclusion: Android's modular design ensures flexibility, portability, and efficient resource utilization.

Chapter 5: Most Asked Important Questions - Part B

Q.1. What is process scheduling? Explain various scheduling criteria used to evaluate CPU scheduling algorithms.

Answer: Process scheduling is the mechanism by which the operating system decides which process in the ready queue is to be allocated the CPU for execution. It is a fundamental aspect of multiprogramming systems where multiple processes compete for CPU time. The main objective of process scheduling is to optimize CPU utilization, response time, throughput, and turnaround time, ensuring fairness among all processes. Various scheduling criteria are used to evaluate scheduling algorithms. CPU utilization measures how effectively the CPU is kept busy. Throughput refers to the number of processes completed in a unit of time. Turnaround time is the total time taken from process submission to completion. Waiting time is the total time a process spends in the ready queue. Response time is the time from process submission to the first response produced. Additionally, fairness ensures that no process is starved for CPU time. An effective scheduling algorithm strikes a balance among these criteria to meet system goals.

Q.2. Define real-time operating systems. Explain hard real-time and soft real-time systems with suitable examples.

Answer: A real-time operating system (RTOS) is designed to process data and events within a strict time constraint. It guarantees a predictable response to external events and ensures that critical tasks are completed within their deadlines. In hard real-time systems, missing a deadline can lead to catastrophic consequences, as these systems are used in mission-critical environments such as medical devices, avionics, and nuclear power plants. For example, in a pacemaker, a missed deadline could be fatal. In contrast, soft real-time systems tolerate occasional deadline misses without severe consequences, although performance may degrade. Examples include multimedia systems and online transaction processing. RTOS prioritizes predictability over throughput and implements specialized scheduling algorithms to ensure deterministic behavior.

Q.3. What is process synchronization? Explain why synchronization is important in multiprogramming environments.

Answer: Process synchronization refers to the coordination of concurrent processes to ensure correct and predictable outcomes when accessing shared resources. In multiprogramming environments, multiple processes often require access to common data structures such as buffers, variables, or files. Without proper synchronization, race conditions can occur, leading to inconsistent or erroneous results. Synchronization mechanisms like semaphores, monitors, and mutex locks prevent such conflicts by allowing only one process to access the critical section at a time. For instance, in a producer-consumer problem, synchronization ensures that the producer does not overwrite data before the consumer reads it and that the consumer does not attempt to consume data that has not yet been produced. Thus, synchronization plays a vital role in maintaining data integrity and system stability.

Q.4. Describe virtual memory. How does it allow execution of programs larger than the physical memory?

Answer: Virtual memory is a memory management technique that allows the execution of processes that may not be entirely resident in physical memory. It provides an abstraction where each process appears to have a large, continuous block of memory, even though the underlying physical memory may be smaller and fragmented. This is achieved through techniques like paging and segmentation, where only the active portions of a process are loaded into RAM while the rest remains on secondary storage (such as a hard disk). When a process references a part of memory that is not in RAM, a page fault occurs, and the operating system loads the required page from disk into memory. This approach not only enables running large programs but also improves multiprogramming by allowing multiple processes to coexist in memory without interfering with each other.

Q.5. Explain the concept of demand paging. Discuss the advantages and disadvantages of demand paging.

Answer: Demand paging is a virtual memory technique where pages of a process are loaded into physical memory only when they are referenced, rather than preloading all pages at process startup. When a process tries to access a page not in RAM, a page fault occurs, and the operating system loads the required page from disk into memory. This approach reduces the amount of memory needed and allows more processes to be accommodated simultaneously. The primary advantage of demand paging is its efficient use of memory, as only necessary pages are loaded. It also improves system responsiveness for large programs. However, the technique has disadvantages such as increased page fault overhead and the possibility of thrashing if the system is overloaded with active processes, leading to excessive swapping of pages between memory and disk.

Q.6. Explain the Banker's algorithm for deadlock avoidance in detail with an example.

Answer: The Banker's algorithm is a resource allocation strategy used to avoid deadlocks by ensuring that the system never enters an unsafe state. It works by evaluating every resource request and granting it only if it leads to a safe state where all processes can eventually complete their execution. The algorithm maintains data structures like Available, Max, Allocation, and Need matrices to keep track of resource distribution. When a process requests resources, the system simulates granting the request and checks if a safe sequence exists for all processes. If such a sequence exists, the resources are allocated; otherwise, the request is denied. For example, consider three processes and three types of resources. The algorithm determines whether granting a request allows all processes to complete without circular waiting. If so, the system remains deadlock-free.

Q.7. Describe the architecture of UNIX operating system. Explain the role of the kernel and shell.

Answer: The UNIX operating system has a layered architecture consisting of the hardware layer, the kernel, and user interfaces like the shell. The kernel is the core component responsible for managing hardware resources, including CPU scheduling, memory management, file systems, and device drivers. It provides system calls for communication between user applications and hardware. The shell serves as a command-line interpreter, allowing users to interact with the system by entering commands that are translated into system calls. Above the shell are application programs and utilities that provide additional functionality. The kernel ensures process isolation and security, while the shell provides a user-friendly interface for executing programs, managing files, and performing administrative tasks.

Q.8. Explain the concept of paging and page replacement. Discuss the Least Recently Used (LRU) page replacement algorithm.

Answer: Paging is a memory management technique where physical memory is divided into fixed-size blocks called frames, and logical memory is divided into blocks of the same size called pages. A page table maps virtual pages to physical frames, enabling the CPU to translate virtual addresses into physical ones. When a process references a page not present in memory, a page fault occurs, prompting the operating system to load the required page from secondary storage into RAM. If the physical memory is full, a page replacement algorithm is used to decide which page to evict. The Least Recently Used (LRU) algorithm replaces the page that has not been accessed for the longest time. It assumes that pages used recently will likely be used again soon, reducing the chance of replacing needed pages. LRU can be implemented using counters or stack-based structures but requires maintaining usage history, which adds to system overhead.

Q. 9. What is process control block (PCB)? Explain its components and significance in process management.

Answer:

The process control block (PCB) is a critical data structure maintained by the operating system to store all essential information about a process. It acts as a repository for process attributes, enabling the OS to switch between processes efficiently. Components of a PCB include the process ID, process state (new, ready, running, waiting, terminated), CPU register contents, program counter, memory management information (such as page tables or segment tables), accounting information, and I/O status. When the operating system performs context switching, the PCB saves the current state of a running process and restores the state of another process. This allows multiple processes to share the CPU effectively without data corruption or inconsistency. The PCB is fundamental to multitasking and process isolation, ensuring that each process operates securely and independently.

Q.10. What is thrashing in operating systems? Explain how it occurs and suggest methods to avoid thrashing.

Answer: Thrashing occurs when a system spends more time swapping pages in and out of memory than executing actual processes, resulting in severely degraded performance. It typically happens when the degree of multiprogramming exceeds the system's physical memory capacity, leading to frequent page faults. As processes compete for limited memory, the system continuously replaces pages, many of which are needed again almost immediately. To prevent thrashing, the operating system can implement the working set model, which keeps track of the set of pages a process actively uses and ensures that these pages are resident in memory. Another method is to use page fault frequency (PFF) monitoring to adjust the number of active processes dynamically. If the page fault rate exceeds a certain threshold, the OS can reduce the degree of multiprogramming by suspending or swapping out processes. Increasing physical memory and using better page replacement algorithms also help in mitigating thrashing.

Q. 11. Describe the architecture of the Linux operating system in detail.

Answer: The Linux operating system follows a layered monolithic kernel architecture that combines modularity and high performance. At the core lies the kernel, which is responsible for managing hardware resources such as the CPU, memory, and I/O devices. The kernel provides essential services like process scheduling, memory management, file system operations, device driver management, and networking. Above the kernel, system libraries offer standard functions that abstract kernel-level complexities, enabling application developers to interact with the OS without dealing with hardware details. The user space contains applications and utilities, including shells and graphical interfaces, through which users interact with the system. The modularity of the Linux kernel allows dynamically loading or unloading components like device drivers at runtime, enhancing flexibility and scalability. This architecture supports multitasking, multiuser operations, and robust security mechanisms, making Linux suitable for servers, desktops, and embedded systems.

Q.12. What is the role of the operating system in file management? Explain the various operations performed on files.

Answer: The operating system plays a central role in managing files on storage devices, providing a logical view of data and abstracting hardware complexities. It maintains file systems that organize data into files and directories, allowing users and programs to store and retrieve information efficiently. Common file operations performed by the OS include creating new files, opening existing files for reading or writing, reading data from or writing data to files, appending data, and closing files once operations are complete. The OS also supports operations like renaming, deleting, copying, and moving files. It enforces access permissions and protection mechanisms to ensure data security and integrity in multiuser environments. Additionally, the OS handles storage allocation, mapping logical file structures to physical disk blocks, and managing free space to optimize storage utilization.

Q.13. Explain the concept of device management in operating systems. How does the OS handle different types of devices?

Answer: Device management in an operating system involves controlling and coordinating hardware devices to ensure efficient and error-free operation. The OS abstracts hardware details, presenting a uniform interface for applications to interact with devices. Devices are broadly classified into character devices, which transfer data one character at a time (e.g., keyboards, serial ports), and block devices, which transfer data in fixed-size blocks (e.g., hard drives). The OS uses device drivers as intermediaries to translate high-level commands into device-specific instructions. It also implements buffering to accommodate speed differences between devices and the CPU, caching to improve access times, and spooling to manage slower devices like printers. The OS schedules I/O operations, prioritizing requests and preventing conflicts in multiuser systems. Error detection and recovery mechanisms are integrated to handle device failures and ensure system reliability.

Q.14. What is a semaphore? Explain how semaphores are used to solve the producer-consumer problem.

Answer: A semaphore is a synchronization primitive used in operating systems to control access to shared resources and prevent race conditions. It is an integer variable that can only be accessed through two atomic operations: wait (also called P or down) and signal (also called V or up). In the producer-consumer problem, semaphores are used to coordinate the actions of producer and consumer processes that share a bounded buffer. Three semaphores are typically employed: mutex for mutual exclusion, empty to count empty slots, and full to count filled slots. The producer process performs a wait operation on the empty semaphore before adding an item to the buffer and signals the full semaphore afterward. The consumer process waits on the full semaphore before consuming an item and signals the empty semaphore after removing the item. This synchronization ensures that producers do not overwrite data in a full buffer and consumers do not attempt to read from an empty buffer.

Q.15. Explain the concept of process states. Describe process state transitions with the help of a diagram.

Answer:

A process in an operating system goes through various states during its lifetime. The major process states are New, Ready, Running, Waiting (or Blocked), and Terminated. When a process is first created, it is in the New state. Once it is admitted into the ready queue, it enters the Ready state, waiting for CPU allocation. When the scheduler selects it, the process transitions to the Running state. If the process requires I/O or an event to occur, it moves to the Waiting state until the event completes. Once the event is completed, the process returns to the Ready state. After completing its execution, the process enters the Terminated state. These transitions are managed by the operating system to ensure proper coordination between processes. A state transition diagram visually represents these movements, showing arrows between states such as Ready to Running (when dispatched) or Running to Waiting (when an I/O request occurs). This model helps in understanding process scheduling and management.

Q.16. What is a file system? Explain the different types of file systems with examples.

Answer: A file system is a method and data structure used by operating systems to control how data is stored, organized, and retrieved from storage devices. It provides an abstraction that allows users to create, modify, delete, and organize files in directories. Common types of file systems include FAT (File Allocation Table), NTFS (New Technology File System), ext3/ext4 (Extended File System used in Linux), and HFS+ (used in macOS). FAT is a simple file system widely used in USB drives and memory cards, but it lacks support for advanced features like permissions. NTFS supports file permissions, encryption, and journaling for better reliability. The ext3 and ext4 file systems are journaled file systems used in Linux, providing efficient storage and recovery mechanisms. The choice of file system affects performance, security, and compatibility across platforms.

Q.17. Explain the concept of memory fragmentation. Differentiate between internal and external fragmentation with examples.

Answer: Memory fragmentation occurs when free memory is divided into small pieces and cannot be used efficiently, leading to wasted space. Internal fragmentation happens when memory is allocated in fixed-size blocks, and the requested memory is smaller than the block size, leaving unused space within the block. For example, if a process requests 6KB and the block size is 8KB,

2KB is wasted internally. External fragmentation occurs when there is enough total free memory, but it is scattered in small chunks, preventing allocation to processes that require larger contiguous memory blocks. For example, if free memory exists as 3KB, 4KB, and 2KB chunks, a request for 8KB cannot be satisfied despite having 9KB free. Techniques like paging and compaction help minimize fragmentation.

Q.18. Describe the architecture of Android operating system in detail.

Answer: Android is a Linux-based mobile operating system with a layered architecture designed for flexibility and portability. At the base is the Linux kernel, which provides core system services such as memory management, process management, and device drivers. Above the kernel are native libraries, including WebKit for browser functionality, SQLite for databases, and OpenGL for graphics rendering. The Android Runtime (ART) executes applications using ahead-of-time compilation for improved performance. The application framework layer provides APIs for developers to manage activities, resources, and content providers. At the top are user applications, such as the dialer, browser, and user-installed apps. This architecture allows hardware abstraction and supports a wide range of devices while maintaining a secure and modular design.

Q.19. What is direct memory access (DMA)? Explain how DMA improves system performance.

Answer: Direct memory access (DMA) is a method that allows peripheral devices to transfer data directly to and from memory without involving the CPU for each byte of transfer. In traditional programmed I/O, the CPU is responsible for moving data, which wastes processing time on repetitive tasks. With DMA, the CPU initializes the transfer by specifying the source, destination, and size of the data. The DMA controller then handles the transfer, freeing the CPU to perform other computations. Once the transfer is complete, the DMA controller sends an interrupt to inform the CPU. This approach significantly improves system performance, particularly for high-speed devices like disks and network cards, by reducing CPU overhead and increasing data throughput.

Q.20. Explain disk scheduling algorithms. Describe the SCAN and C-SCAN algorithms with examples.

Answer: Disk scheduling algorithms determine the order in which I/O requests to a disk are serviced to minimize seek time and improve performance. The SCAN algorithm, also known as the elevator algorithm, moves the disk arm in one direction, servicing all requests in its path until it reaches the end of the disk. It then reverses direction and services requests in the opposite direction. For example, with requests at tracks 40, 10, 90, and 50, if the head starts at track 30 moving upward, SCAN services 40, 50, and 90 before reversing to service 10. The C-SCAN (Circular SCAN) algorithm operates similarly but only services requests in one direction. When the head reaches the end, it returns to the beginning without servicing requests during the return. This provides a more uniform wait time for requests. Both algorithms reduce seek time compared to first-come-first-serve (FCFS) scheduling.

Q.21. What is virtual memory? Discuss how paging and segmentation support virtual memory.

Answer: Virtual memory is a technique that allows execution of processes that may not fit entirely into physical memory by using secondary storage as an extension of RAM. Paging supports virtual memory by dividing both logical and physical memory into fixed-size blocks called pages and frames, respectively. When a page needed by a process is not in RAM, the operating system brings it from disk to memory, allowing processes to execute even if only part of them is loaded. Segmentation, on the other hand, divides memory into variable-sized segments based on logical divisions such as code, data, and stack. The OS maps logical segment addresses to physical memory locations and swaps segments in and out as required. Together, paging and segmentation make efficient use of memory and support protection and sharing in multiprogramming environments.

22. Explain the concept of process synchronization and describe how Peterson's algorithm provides a solution for two processes.

Answer:

Process synchronization is the coordination of concurrent processes to ensure they do not interfere with each other while accessing shared resources. Without synchronization, processes may experience race conditions, leading to incorrect results. Peterson's algorithm provides a software solution to achieve mutual exclusion between two processes. It uses two shared variables: a boolean array to indicate interest in entering the critical section and a turn variable to decide whose turn it is to enter. When a process wants to enter its critical section, it sets its flag to true and assigns the turn to the other process. It then waits until the other process is not interested or until it is its turn. This algorithm ensures mutual exclusion, progress, and bounded waiting, making it a reliable synchronization technique in environments without hardware support for atomic operations.

Q.23. What is spooling? Explain how spooling improves system performance with an example.

Answer: Spooling, which stands for Simultaneous Peripheral Operations On-Line, is a technique used by operating systems to manage input and output operations efficiently. In spooling, data destined for an I/O device is temporarily stored on secondary storage, such as a disk, and is later sent to the device at its own pace. This approach allows the CPU and other processes to continue working without waiting for slow devices like printers to finish their tasks. For example, when multiple users send print jobs to a printer, the operating system stores the jobs in a spool queue on disk. The printer then processes these jobs one by one. Spooling improves system performance by overlapping computation with I/O operations and ensuring better utilization of system resources.

Q.24. Describe the architecture of Windows operating system in detail.

Answer: The Windows operating system uses a hybrid architecture that combines features of monolithic and microkernel designs. At the lowest level is the Hardware Abstraction Layer (HAL), which provides a consistent interface for hardware access and shields higher layers from hardware-specific details. Above the HAL is the kernel, which manages core system functions such as process scheduling, memory management, and interrupt handling. The executive layer offers services like file systems, device drivers, and networking. In user mode, environment subsystems such as Win32, POSIX, and OS/2 provide APIs for application compatibility. The graphical subsystem supports user interfaces and desktop environments. This modular architecture enhances portability, security, and multitasking, making Windows suitable for both personal and enterprise-level computing.

Q.25. Explain the concept of inter-process communication (IPC). Describe shared memory and message passing mechanisms in detail.

Answer: Inter-process communication (IPC) is a mechanism that allows processes to exchange data and coordinate their actions in a multitasking environment. IPC is crucial for building distributed systems and enabling collaboration between concurrent processes. Shared memory is an IPC technique where multiple processes share a region of physical memory. Processes can directly read from and write to the shared memory area, making communication fast and efficient. However, it requires explicit synchronization mechanisms like semaphores to avoid race conditions. Message passing is another IPC method where processes communicate by sending and receiving messages using system calls. This approach is safer as processes do not share memory, but it involves kernel intervention, which can add overhead. Message passing can be synchronous, where the sender waits for acknowledgment, or asynchronous, where the sender continues execution after sending the message.

Q.26. What is context switching? Explain the steps involved in context switching and its overhead.

Answer: Context switching is the process of storing the state of a currently running process so that another process can be executed. It allows multitasking by enabling the CPU to switch between processes. During a context switch, the operating system saves the current process's state, including its program counter, CPU registers, and memory management information, into its process control block (PCB). The OS then loads the state of the next process to resume its execution. While context switching is essential for multitasking, it introduces overhead because no useful work is done during the switch. Frequent context switches can degrade system performance, particularly in systems with high process scheduling rates.

Q.27. Explain the concept of disk fragmentation. How can fragmentation be minimized or removed?

Answer: Disk fragmentation occurs when files are divided into non-contiguous blocks on the disk, leading to increased seek time during file access. Fragmentation happens over time as files are created, modified, and deleted, leaving small gaps that are too small for new files. This results in slower performance because the disk head must move to multiple locations to read a single file.

Fragmentation can be minimized by using allocation techniques like contiguous allocation or extent-based allocation. To remove existing fragmentation, utilities like disk defragmenters rearrange file blocks on the disk to store them contiguously. Modern file systems such as NTFS and ext4 include features that reduce fragmentation by design.

Q.28. What is the difference between blocking and non-blocking I/O? Explain with examples.

Answer: Blocking I/O and non-blocking I/O are two approaches to handling input/output operations in operating systems. In blocking I/O, the process requesting I/O is suspended until the operation completes. For example, when a program reads from a file, it waits until the data is fully read before resuming execution. This approach is simple but can lead to CPU idle time if the device is slow. In non-blocking I/O, the process does not wait for the I/O operation to complete; instead, it continues execution and checks later whether the operation succeeded. This method improves CPU utilization by allowing the process to perform other tasks while waiting for I/O. Non-blocking I/O is widely used in network programming to handle multiple connections simultaneously.

Q.29. Explain the difference between user-level threads and kernel-level threads. Why are hybrid threading models used?

Answer: User-level threads are managed by a user-space library, and the operating system kernel is unaware of them. These threads are lightweight and offer fast context switching, but if one thread performs a blocking system call, the entire process is blocked. Kernel-level threads, on the other hand, are managed by the operating system, and each thread is individually scheduled. They allow better concurrency on multiprocessor systems but incur higher overhead due to kernel involvement in thread management. Hybrid threading models combine the advantages of both approaches by using user-level threads mapped to a smaller number of kernel threads. This model provides flexibility and efficiency in applications requiring high levels of concurrency.

Q.30. What are file access methods? Explain sequential, direct, and indexed access in detail with examples.

Answer: File access methods define how data within a file can be read or written. In sequential access, data is accessed in order, starting from the beginning of the file. For example, tape drives support only sequential access. This method is simple but inefficient for random access. In direct access, data blocks can be read or written in any order using their addresses. Hard disks support direct access, enabling operations like updating a specific database record. Indexed access uses an index to store pointers to file blocks, allowing both sequential and random access. For instance, a library catalog system may use an index to quickly locate book records. Indexed access provides flexibility but adds overhead for maintaining the index.

Q.31. What is the difference between multiprogramming, multitasking, and multiprocessing? Explain with examples.

Answer: Multiprogramming is a technique where multiple programs reside in memory, and the operating system switches the CPU between them to maximize utilization. For example, while one program waits for I/O, another can use the CPU. Multitasking is a refinement of multiprogramming where the CPU switches rapidly between tasks, giving the illusion that they run simultaneously. Modern operating systems like Windows and Linux support multitasking. Multiprocessing involves using multiple CPUs to execute processes in parallel, improving performance for compute-intensive applications. High-performance servers and supercomputers use multiprocessing to handle large workloads efficiently.

Q.32. Describe the Readers-Writers problem and provide a solution using semaphores.

Answer: The Readers-Writers problem arises when multiple processes access a shared resource such as a file. Readers can access the resource concurrently, but writers require exclusive access to prevent data inconsistency. To solve this problem, semaphores can be used to synchronize readers and writers. A semaphore for mutual exclusion ensures only one writer accesses the resource at a time, while a counter tracks active readers. Before reading, a process increments the reader count and waits if a writer is active. When done, it decrements the count. Writers wait until there are no active readers before writing. This solution prevents race conditions and ensures data integrity.

Q.33. Explain memory allocation techniques. Describe first-fit, best-fit, and worst-fit methods with examples.

Answer: Memory allocation techniques determine how free memory is assigned to processes. In the first-fit method, the system allocates the first available block that is large enough for the process. This method is simple but may leave small unusable gaps. In best-fit allocation, the system assigns the smallest free block that meets the process's needs, minimizing wasted space but potentially increasing allocation time. Worst-fit allocates the largest available block, leaving larger gaps that may accommodate future requests. For example, if free memory blocks are 100KB, 500KB, and 200KB, and a process requests 180KB, best-fit chooses 200KB, first-fit may choose 200KB or 500KB, and worst-fit chooses 500KB.

Q.34. What are page replacement algorithms? Explain FIFO and Optimal page replacement in detail.

Answer: Page replacement algorithms determine which memory page to evict when a page fault occurs, and physical memory is full. The FIFO (First-In-First-Out) algorithm replaces the oldest page in memory. While simple, it suffers from Belady's anomaly, where increasing the number of frames may lead to more page faults. Optimal page replacement evicts the page that will not be used for the longest time in the future, achieving the lowest possible page fault rate. However, it requires knowledge of future memory references, making it impractical for real systems. These algorithms balance memory utilization and performance in virtual memory management.

Q.35. Explain the concept of segmentation in memory management. How does segmentation differ from paging?

Answer: Segmentation is a memory management technique where the logical address space of a process is divided into variable-sized segments based on the logical divisions of a program, such as code, data, stack, and heap. Each segment has its own base and limit, which define the starting address and length of the segment in memory. The operating system maintains a segment table for each process, which stores the base address and limit of each segment. When a process generates a logical address, it is divided into a segment number and offset, which the memory management unit (MMU) translates into a physical address. Segmentation allows protection and sharing at the segment level, as each segment can have its own access rights. Unlike paging, where memory is divided into fixed-size blocks, segmentation uses variable sizes, which avoids internal fragmentation but can lead to external fragmentation. Segmentation is better suited for programs with distinct logical divisions, while paging simplifies memory allocation by using fixed-size pages.

Q.36. What is a device driver? Explain the role of device drivers in operating systems.

Answer: A device driver is a specialized software component that acts as an interface between the operating system and hardware devices. Device drivers translate generic operating system commands into device-specific instructions, enabling applications to interact with hardware without needing to know its details. When a program requests an I/O operation, such as reading from a disk or printing a document, the OS passes the request to the relevant device driver, which communicates directly with the hardware. Device drivers handle operations like initialization, data transfer, and error management for the device. They also provide abstraction, allowing hardware changes without requiring modifications to higher-level software. For example, a printer driver enables printing functionality regardless of the printer model. This modular design improves system flexibility and supports hardware compatibility across platforms.

Q.37. Explain the concept of system calls. How do system calls enable communication between user programs and the operating system?

Answer: System calls are the primary mechanism through which user programs request services from the operating system. They provide a controlled interface that allows user applications to access hardware and OS resources safely and securely. When a program needs to perform an operation such as creating a file, allocating memory, or sending data over a network, it cannot access hardware directly due to protection mechanisms. Instead, it issues a system call, which transitions the CPU from user mode to kernel mode, granting the OS permission to execute the requested service. Once the operation completes, control returns to user mode. Common system call categories include process control (e.g., fork, exec), file management (e.g., open, read, write), device management (e.g., ioctl), and communication (e.g., send, receive). System calls abstract hardware complexities, ensuring portability and protection in multitasking environments.

Q.38. What is the difference between preemptive and non-preemptive scheduling? Explain with examples.

Answer: Preemptive scheduling allows the operating system to interrupt a running process and allocate the CPU to another process, ensuring better responsiveness and fair resource distribution. In contrast, non-preemptive scheduling does not allow a running process to be interrupted; it continues execution until it completes or voluntarily gives up the CPU. For example, in preemptive scheduling, if a high-priority process arrives while a lower-priority process is running, the OS suspends the current process and switches to the high-priority one. Algorithms like Round Robin and Priority Scheduling are preemptive. Non-preemptive scheduling, such as First-Come-First-Serve (FCFS) and Shortest Job Next (SJN), may lead to poor responsiveness if a long process blocks shorter ones. Preemptive scheduling is more suitable for time-sharing systems, while non-preemptive scheduling simplifies process management but may cause delays.

Q.39. Explain the concept of deadlock detection and recovery. How does the operating system handle deadlocks?

Answer: Deadlock detection and recovery are techniques used by the operating system to handle situations where processes are stuck waiting for resources held by each other, forming a circular wait. Deadlock detection involves monitoring resource allocation and determining whether a deadlock has occurred. One common method is to use a resource allocation graph (RAG) and check for cycles, which indicate a deadlock in systems with single resource instances. For systems with multiple resource instances, algorithms like the Banker's algorithm can be extended to detect unsafe states. Once a deadlock is detected, the OS can recover by aborting one or more processes to break the circular wait or by preempting resources from processes and reallocating them. The choice of which process to terminate or preempt depends on factors like priority, resource usage, and execution progress. Deadlock detection and recovery are often used in systems where preventing deadlocks is too restrictive or impractical.

Q.40. What are the goals and functions of an operating system? Explain in detail.

Answer: The primary goals of an operating system are to manage hardware resources efficiently, provide an environment for executing programs, and offer user-friendly interfaces for interaction. It acts as an intermediary between users and hardware, enabling multitasking, resource sharing, and system security. Key functions of an operating system include process management, which involves creating, scheduling, and terminating processes; memory management, which allocates and deallocates memory for programs while ensuring protection and efficient utilization; and file system management, which organizes and controls access to data stored on disks. The OS also manages devices through drivers, handles input/output operations, and provides network connectivity. Security and protection mechanisms prevent unauthorized access to system resources. Additionally, the OS provides user interfaces such as command-line interpreters or graphical user interfaces, allowing users to interact with the system easily. These functions together ensure optimal system performance and user convenience.

9 789369 914333

Printed at Repro India Ltd.